An Educational

Read and Color

Book of

SHARKS

EDITOR
Linda Spizzirri

ILLUSTRATION
Peter M. Spizzirri

COVER ART
Peter M. Spizzirri

CONTENTS

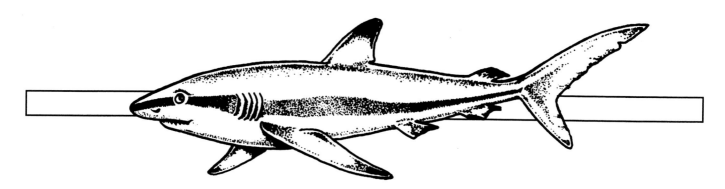

NAME: TIGER SHARK (*Galeocerdo cuvieri*)

WHERE IT IS FOUND: IN TROPICAL AND SUBTROPICAL SEAS WORLD WIDE. SEVERAL HAVE BEEN TAKEN IN COLDER WATERS OF ICELAND AND MASSACHUSETTS.

WHERE IT LIVES: TIGER SHARKS HAVE BEEN FOUND BOTH OFFSHORE IN OPEN OCEANS AS WELL AS QUITE CLOSE TO SHORE, SMALL ISLANDS AND CORAL REEFS.

SIZE: MAY GROW TO LENGTHS OF 12 TO 15 FT.

WHAT IT EATS: FISH

HAS THIS SHARK ATTACKED MAN: Yes. This species has a particularly bad reputation for shark attacks. There are a number of confirmed cases of shark attacks by this shark from Florida, the Bahama Islands, and Central America.

COLOR IT: Small tiger sharks (under 5-6 feet) have a pattern of dark brown bars along the sides over a grey or greyish-brown background color. In adult tiger sharks this barring is either absent or present only on the body in the tail region.

INTERESTING FACTS: The stomach contents of young tiger sharks, as well as adults, include such interesting items as squid, sea turtles, porpoises, lumps of coal, other sharks, sting rays, license plates and other types of assorted garbage.

NAME:	GREENLAND SHARK (*Somniosus microcephalus*)
WHERE IT IS FOUND:	IN COLD NORTHERN SEAS, SOMETIMES IN AREAS PACKED WITH ICE
WHERE IT LIVES:	GREENLAND SHARKS ARE USUALLY FOUND ON THE BOTTOM IN DEEP WATER. SOMETIMES THEY HAVE BEEN SEEN AT THE SURFACE FEEDING ON SMALL FISH
SIZE:	ARE BELIEVED TO REACH LENGTHS OF 12 TO 15 FEET.
WHAT IT EATS:	SMALL FISH. THE COMPLETE DIET OF THE SHARK IS NOT KNOWN
HAS THIS SHARK ATTACKED MAN:	No.
COLOR IT:	Overall body color is either dark brown, grey or blue. The fins and belly are nearly the same color as the body, although sometimes they may be slightly lighter in color.

NAME: THRESHER SHARK
(*Alopias vulpinus*)

WHERE IT IS FOUND: IN MOST TROPICAL, SUBTROPICAL AND TEMPERATE SEAS WORLD WIDE.

WHERE IT LIVES: THRESHER SHARKS ARE USUALLY FOUND IN THE OPEN OCEAN OFFSHORE. THEY WILL COME CLOSE TO SHORE OCCASIONALLY TO FEED ON SCHOOLS OF SMALL FISHES. AT TIMES THEY HAVE BEEN CAUGHT IN VERY DEEP WATER.

SIZE: CAN GROW TO LENGTHS OF 20 FEET, ALTHOUGH SMALLER SIZES ARE MORE COMMON

WHAT IT EATS: MOSTLY SMALL FISH

HAS THIS SHARK ATTACKED MAN: Possibly. There are two unconfirmed reports of thresher shark attacks from New Jersey and South Africa.

COLOR IT: The color may vary from shark to shark. They may be blue, grey, brown or black on the sides of the body, back and fins. The belly is white.

INTERESTING FACTS: Thresher sharks are thought to feed on small fishes by herding them in a small school by using the upper part of the long tail fin.

NAME: SWELL SHARK
                               (*Cephaloscyllium ventriosum*)

WHERE IT IS FOUND: IN THE PACIFIC OCEAN OFF MEXICO
                               AND CALIFORNIA

WHERE IT LIVES: DURING THE DAY SWELL SHARKS LIVE
                               IN SMALL CAVES AND CREVICES ON
                               THE BOTTOM OR IN CORAL REEFS

SIZE: 3 FEET OR MORE

WHAT IT EATS: SWELL SHARKS ARE BELIEVED TO FEED
                               AT NIGHT ON LOBSTER AND SMALL
                               SHELLFISH (CRAB, ETC.)

HAS THIS SHARK
ATTACKED MAN: No.

COLOR IT: Overall body color is brown with dark brown
                               (almost black) saddle-like markings and light
                               spots across the back.

INTERESTING FACTS: When this shark is molested or captured it
                               can inflate its body with water causing it to
                               swell which is how it got its common name.
                               This shark has also been kept alive
                               successfully in public aquariums in
                               California, Chicago and Japan.

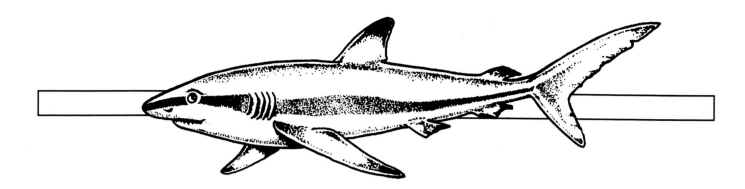

NAME:	GREAT HAMMERHEAD SHARK (*Sphyrna mokarran*)
WHERE IT IS FOUND:	IN ALL TROPICAL SEAS AROUND THE WORLD
WHERE IT LIVES:	IN SHALLOW AND DEEP WATER AND AROUND CORAL REEFS
SIZE:	GREAT HAMMERHEADS HAVE BEEN KNOWN TO ATTAIN LENGTH OF ABOUT 20 FEET
WHAT IT EATS:	FISH
HAS THIS SHARK ATTACKED MAN:	Yes. There are a number of confirmed reports of shark attacks by great hammerheads from Florida, California and New York.
COLOR IT:	Brownish grey or blue-grey on the sides, back and fins and paler shades of these colors on the underside.
INTERESTING FACTS:	There are several species of hammerhead sharks besides the great hammerhead. The function of the hammer shaped head of the hammerhead sharks may be to help the shark see better since the eyes are on the ends of the hammer shaped head.

NAME:	WHITETIP SHARK (*Carcharhinus longimanus*)
WHERE IT IS FOUND:	IN ALL TROPICAL AND SUBTROPICAL SEAS
WHERE IT LIVES:	WHITETIP SHARKS ARE USUALLY FOUND IN THE OPEN OCEAN AND ALSO IN MORE SHALLOW AREAS AROUND CORAL REEFS.
SIZE:	GROW TO LENGTHS OF 11-12 FEET
WHAT IT EATS:	FISH
HAS THIS SHARK ATTACKED MAN:	Yes. There is at least one confirmed case of a shark attack from a whitetip shark from the Caribbean Sea. Other suspected but unconfirmed attacks from this shark have taken place in the Bahama Islands and in Africa.
COLOR IT:	Blue, grey or brown on the sides, back and fins, with white or yellow on the belly. The fins are tipped with white and may also have some greyish mottled (speckled) color.

NAME: WHALE SHARK
(*Rhincodon typus*)

WHERE IT IS FOUND: AROUND THE WORLD IN TROPICAL AND SUBTROPICAL WATERS

WHERE IT LIVES: THIS SHARK SPECIES IS ONLY FOUND OFFSHORE IN THE OPEN OCEAN. ONLY RARELY HAS IT BEEN SEEN NEAR SHORE OR CORAL REEFS

SIZE: COMMON SIZE IS 20 TO 25 FEET BUT THE WHALE SHARK CAN GROW 45 TO 50 FEET IN LENGTH

WHAT IT EATS: THE WHALE SHARK FEEDS ALMOST ENTIRELY ON PLANKTON WHICH IT STRAINS FROM THE WATER WITH SIEVE-LIKE STRAINERS WHICH IT HAS IN ITS JAWS. WHALE SHARKS ALSO FEED ON SMALL FISH AND SHRIMP

HAS THIS SHARK ATTACKED MAN: Usually the whale shark is a peaceful shark in spite of its large size. However, when provoked it has been known to attack boats.

COLOR IT: Dark grey to brown along the sides and back which also have small whitish or yellowish spots. There are also small numerous white or yellow spots on the head, tail and back fin.

INTERESTING FACTS: The whale shark is the largest living shark known to man. It feeds by straining food from water with finger-like filaments (gill rakers) projecting from its gills. The mouth of the whale shark may be up to six feet across. Whale shark teeth are among the smallest of any shark and are seldom, if ever, used in feeding.

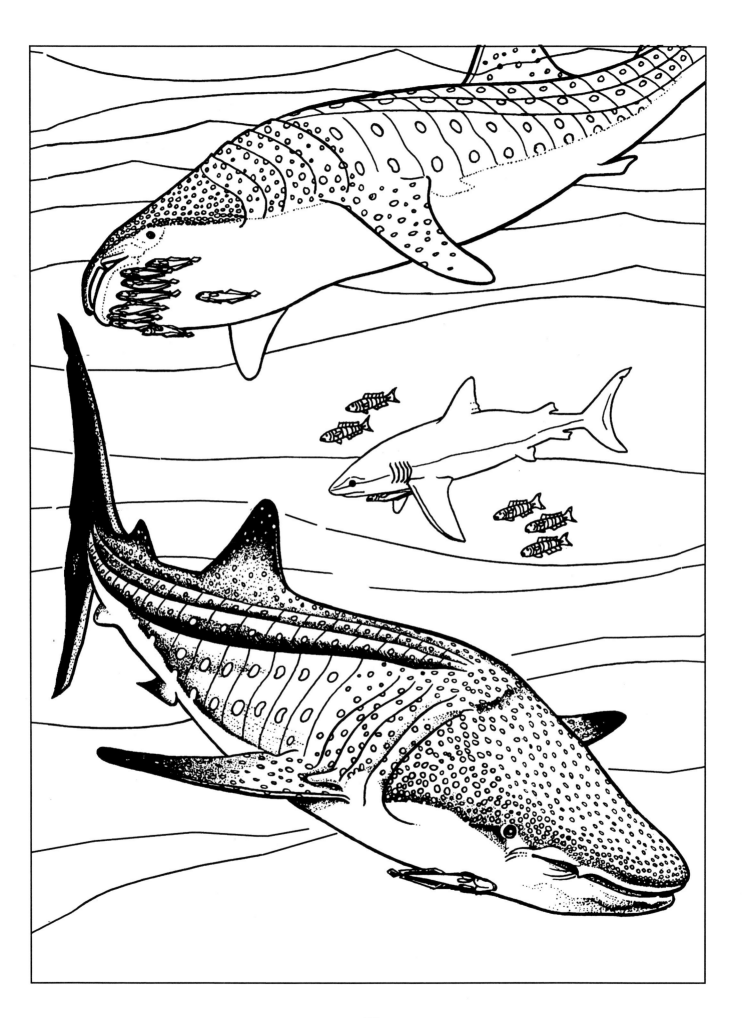

NAME: GREAT WHITE SHARK (*Carcharodon carcharias*) ALSO CALLED MAN-EATER

WHERE IT IS FOUND: IN ALL TROPICAL, SUBTROPICAL AND TEMPERATE SEAS WORLD WIDE

WHERE IT LIVES: GREAT WHITE SHARKS HAVE BEEN FOUND IN THE OPEN OCEAN FAR OFFSHORE, NEAR CORAL REEFS AND IN SHALLOW WATER QUITE CLOSE TO SHORE

SIZE: GROW TO SIZES OF AT LEAST 21 FEET

WHAT IT EATS: FISH, SEALS, SEA LIONS AND ANYTHING ELSE IT CAN POSSIBLY CATCH - INCLUDING OTHER SHARKS

HAS THIS SHARK ATTACKED MAN: Yes. There are numerous reports of great white sharks attacking swimmers and boats along the coast of the United States, Central America, Africa and Australia.

COLOR IT: Grey, greyish-brown or blue on the sides, back and fins, and white on the belly. The tips of the pectoral or shoulder fins and the tips of the dorsal fin (fin on the middle of the back) are tipped with dark (black) color.

INTERESTING FACTS: Like the bull shark, the great white shark has triangular teeth with serrated edges. The edges of the teeth feel like the edge of a hack-saw blade. The great white is the third largest shark known, only the whale shark and basking shark are larger. The great white is the largest fish eating shark, since the whale shark and basking shark feed mainly on plankton.

NAME:	SIX-GILLED SHARK (*Hexanchus griseus*)
WHERE IT IS FOUND:	WORLD-WIDE IN ALL SEAS
WHERE IT LIVES:	SIX-GILLED SHARKS ARE USUALLY FOUND IN VERY DEEP WATER BUT HAVE SOMETIMES BEEN SEEN IN SHALLOW WATER
SIZE:	SIX-GILLED SHARKS ARE BELIEVED TO REACH LENGTHS OF AT LEAST 15 1/2 FEET
WHAT IT EATS:	FISH AND POSSIBLY SMALL MARINE INVERTEBRATES (clams, crabs, etc.)
HAS THIS SHARK ATTACKED MAN:	No.
COLOR IT:	Light brown, dark brown or grey on the sides, back and fins, with lighter shades of these colors on the belly.
INTERESTING FACTS:	Not very much information is available concerning the feeding habits or other general habits of this shark partly because it usually lives in deep water and partly because this shark is not very common.

NAME:	SAND TIGER SHARK (*Odontaspis taurus*)
WHERE IT IS FOUND:	WESTERN ATLANTIC OCEAN TO THE MEDITERRANEAN SEA
WHERE IT LIVES:	SAND SHARKS LIVE ON OR CLOSE TO THE BOTTOM USUALLY IN 30 FEET OF WATER OR LESS, SOMETIMES THEY LIVE IN WATER AS SHALLOW AS 2 TO 6 FEET
SIZE:	SAND SHARKS HAVE BEEN KNOWN TO REACH LENGTHS OF 10 1/2 FEET
WHAT IT EATS:	FISH
HAS THIS SHARK ATTACKED MAN:	Yes. There is at least one confirmed case of a shark attack from a sand shark from South Africa and another from Australia.
COLOR IT:	Overall body color grey or brown on the back, sides and fins with pale white on the belly.

NAME: BLACKTIP SHARK
(*Carcharhinus maculipinnis*)

WHERE IT IS FOUND: THROUGHOUT THE CARIBBEAN SEA. THE COASTS OF FLORIDA, CUBA AND PUERTO RICO

WHERE IT LIVES: LITTLE IS KNOWN CONCERNING WHERE THIS SHARK SPENDS MOST OF ITS TIME, HOWEVER, OTHER CLOSELY RELATED SHARKS ARE FOUND LIVING NEAR CORAL REEFS

SIZE: BLACKTIP SHARKS GROW TO SIZES OVER 8 FEET IN LENGTH

WHAT IT EATS: FISH

HAS THIS SHARK
ATTACKED MAN: Yes. There is one confirmed report of a blacktip shark attacking a swimmer in Florida.

COLOR IT: Grey on the sides, back and fins. White on the belly. There is black at the tips of the shoulder fins and dorsal fin (fin in the middle of the back).

NAME:	LEOPARD SHARK (*Triakis semifasciata*)
WHERE IT IS FOUND:	IN THE EASTERN NORTH PACIFIC OCEAN
WHERE IT LIVES:	COMMONLY FOUND IN SHALLOW WATER AREAS INSHORE AND ALSO AROUND CORAL REEFS
SIZE:	GROW TO LENGTHS OF 3 TO 5 FEET, ALTHOUGH FEMALES ARE USUALLY SMALLER
WHAT IT EATS:	FISH
HAS THIS SHARK ATTACKED MAN:	Yes. There is at least one confirmed attack by a leopard shark from California.
COLOR IT:	Grey on the back, sides and fins with black across bars on the upper sides and additional black spots on the sides.
INTERESTING FACTS:	This shark has been successfully kept alive in many aquariums such as the John G. Shedd Aquarium in Chicago.

NAME:	BULL SHARK (*Carcharhinus leucas*)
WHERE IT IS FOUND:	WESTERN NORTH ATLANTIC FROM NEW YORK SOUTHWARD THROUGHOUT THE BAHAMAS ALONG THE ENTIRE CENTRAL AMERICAN COAST TO BRAZIL
WHERE IT LIVES:	BULL SHARKS ARE FOUND CLOSE TO SHORE, NEAR ISLANDS, NEAR AND IN RIVER MOUTHS, AND OCCASIONALLY QUITE A DISTANCE UP STREAM IN FRESHWATER RIVERS
SIZE:	6 TO 9 FEET IS COMMON, ALTHOUGH BULL SHARKS CAN GROW TO 12 FEET
WHAT IT EATS:	FISH, GARBAGE AND WHATEVER ELSE IT CAN CATCH OR FIND
HAS THIS SHARK ATTACKED MAN:	Yes. There are a number of confirmed reports of bull shark attacks from various places in Africa, Central America, Florida and the Caribbean Sea.
COLOR IT:	Grey above on the sides, back and fins. White on the belly. Young bull sharks may have their fins tipped with black, however, this color is absent in adult sharks.
INTERESTING FACTS:	Bull sharks are able to swim great distances up freshwater rivers. In South America, bull sharks have been caught over 2,000 miles upriver from the ocean. In the United States, a small bull shark was caught near Alton, Illinois in 1937.

NAME:	ZEBRA SHARK (*Stegostoma varium*)
WHERE IT IS FOUND:	WATERS OF THE WESTERN PACIFIC, AUSTRALIA AND THE INDIAN OCEAN
WHERE IT LIVES:	SPENDS MOST OF ITS TIME RESTING ON THE BOTTOM IN THE OPEN OCEAN
SIZE:	REACHES LENGTHS OF 11 TO 12 FEET
WHAT IT EATS:	FISH AND INVERTEBRATES
HAS THIS SHARK ATTACKED MAN:	No.
COLOR IT:	Yellowish white overall with dark brown spots.
INTERESTING FACTS:	The name "zebra shark" seems very inappropriate for a spotted shark. The name was probably first applied to the young zebra shark, which is dark brown with white stripes.

NAME: NURSE SHARK
(*Ginglymostoma cirratum*)

WHERE IT IS FOUND: IN THE TROPICAL AND SUBTROPICAL ATLANTIC OCEAN FROM RHODE ISLAND SOUTHWARD TO BRAZIL, AND IN THE TROPICAL AND SUBTROPICAL PACIFIC FROM OREGON TO ECUADOR IN SOUTH AMERICA

WHERE IT LIVES: COMMONLY FOUND LYING ON THE BOTTOM IN ROCKY OR SANDY AREA AND NEAR CORAL REEF AREAS

SIZE: GROW TO LENGTHS OF AT LEAST 14 FEET

WHAT IT EATS: FISH AND INVERTEBRATES (CRABS, ETC.)

HAS THIS SHARK
ATTACKED MAN: Yes, but usually only after being provoked.

COLOR IT: This shark is an overall brown color. The young are also a uniform brown color but they may also be covered with small brown or black spots.

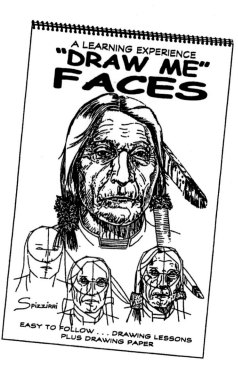